Flicker Flash

To Mom and Dad
Jim, Heather, and Aimee
family and friends
especially Shirley, Jane, Pat, and Mona—
thank you for lighting my way
—J. B. G.

To my parents
Thank you for encouraging me to follow my star.
—N. D.

www.houghtonmifflinbooks.com

Library of Congress Cataloging-in-Publication Data

Graham, Joan Bransfield.
Flicker flash / Joan Bransfield Graham ; illustrated by Nancy Davis.
p. cm.
Summary: A collection of poems celebrating light in its various forms, from candles and
lamps to lightning and fireflies.
RNF ISBN 0-395-90501-X   PAP ISBN 0-618-31102-5
1. Light — Juvenile poetry. 2. Children's poetry, American. [1. Light — Poetry. 2. American
poetry.] I. Davis, Nancy, 1949–   ill. II. Title.
PS3557.R213F55   1999·
811'.54 — dc21   98-12956 CIP AC

Manufactured in the United States of America
BVG 10 9 8 7 6

Flicker Flash

poems by Joan Bransfield Graham
illustrated by Nancy Davis

Light

Light,
 light,
  stretch
  my sight,
   bend back
   c o r n e r s
    of the night.
    Flicker, flash,
     near and far,
      turn on lamps,
       & sprinkle stars.
       One small flame,
        a tiny spark . . .
         or wide as day,
          you scatter dark.

Sun

"From
93,000,000
miles away I bring
you this dynamite, ring-
a-ding day. I'll shout in
your window and bounce
near your head to solar
power you out of
your bed!"

Candle

You
promise quick,
exotic light,
a dancing
vision of
the night,
you give
the room
a painted
face that
blinks and
winks and
helps erase
the feeling
of the empty
black that's
slyly creeping
up my back.

earth **summer t**

is spinning
toward the light,
first it's day,
and then it's
night

around the sun

Firefly

Firefly, flit high then low, do you know what makes you glow?

Crescent Moon

new

grin

moon

night

sliver

the

thin

see

nice to

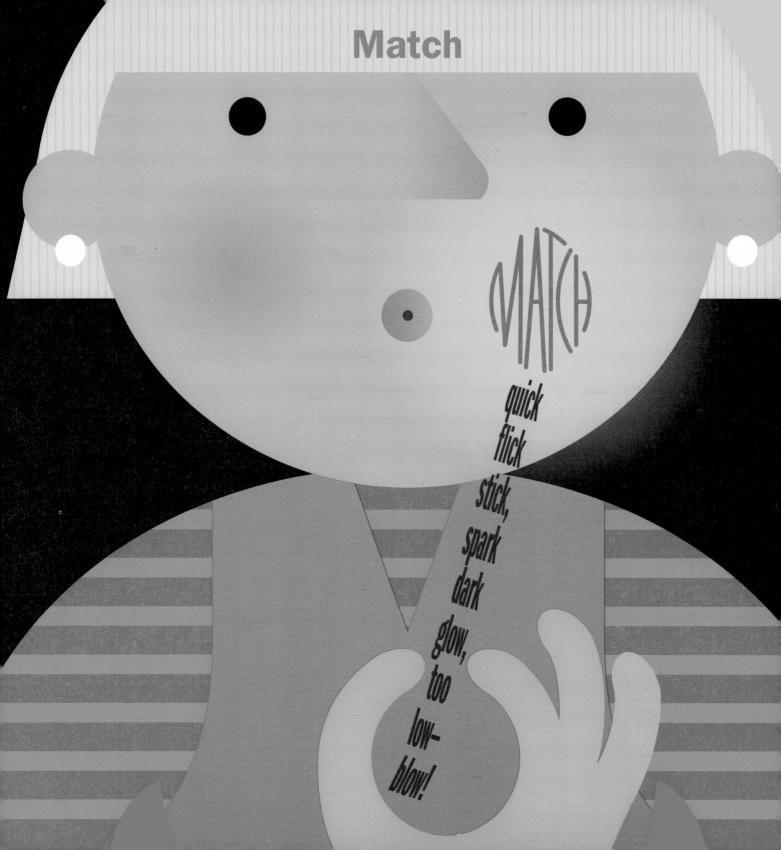

MATCH
quick
flick
stick,
spark
dark
glow,
too
low—
blow!

Birthday Candles

Happy Day Happy Year

Like shooting stars
that blaze the dark,
you flame — then
disappear. But when
I look, I see your light
in faces, circled near.

Light Bulb

Thomas
Edison didn't
hesitate to let
ideas incubate, and
try again, if they
weren't right. One
day to his intense
delight, he squeezed
his thoughts
into a bulb
and then
turned
on the
light
light
light
!!!

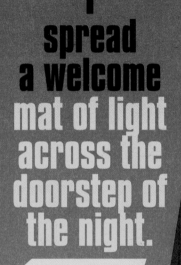

I
spread
a welcome
mat of light
across the
doorstep of
the night.

WELCOME WELCOME
WE MEET AGAIN
WELCOME WELCOME
PLEASE COME IN

Stars

in
space

star
mail

can
seem

quite
slow

this card
was sent

Full Moon

like
a *MIRROR*,
far away, moon
REFLECTS the
flames of day, in
a *SILVER* kind
of way

ago

light
years

a luminous square box brings light through wires and air, shows superheroes save the world while I'm just s i t t i n g there

Refrigerator Light

Open the door.

By
the
light
in the
refrigerator,
I can plainly see
that the Brussels
sprouts are meant
for Y O U . . . the
chocolate cake's
for ME.

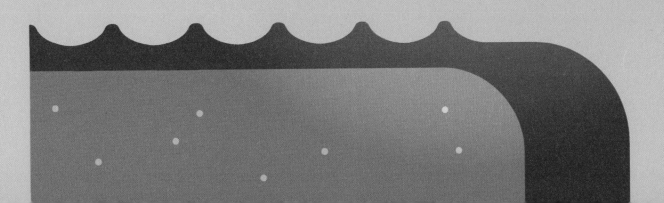

Lighthouse

LIG

LIGHT LIGHT

Oh, Captain of the midnight sky, you stretch your arms and flash your eye across the waves and churning foam to steer me, guide me, safely HOME.

LIGHT HOUSE

FLASH

OPEN THE SHUTTER
SUNLIGHT WILL SPILL
ONTO MY FILM
TO MAKE TIME
STAND STILL

Incubator Bulb

Warm
as a hen,
this toasty
trick will turn
an egg into
a chick!

**PEEP
PEEP**

Flashlight

click
one flick
I am the SUN,
I chase the shadows
one by one, growing scary,
jagged, tall – with brilliant beams
I'll MELT them ALL!

Fireworks

Who plants the star flowers

shooting up high, scattering across the sky petals?

Lamp

soft gold
lamp-shine makes
this book *all mine*, in
this welcome curve of light,
nestled in the lap of night

L
A
M
P
L A M P